THE GOOD GOLF GUIDE

DRIVING FOR DISTANCE

This material previously appeared in *Improve Your Golf*.
This volume compiled by Paul Foston and Sally Hiller.

CLB 3294
© Eaglemoss Publications Ltd 1989, 1990, 1991, 1992

This edition published in 1995 by SMITHMARK Publishers,
a division of U.S. Media Holdings, Inc.,
16 East 32nd Street, New York NY 10016

SMITHMARK books are available for bulk purchase for sales promotion and
premium use. For details write or call the manager of special sales,
SMITHMARK Publishers, Inc.
16 East 32nd Street, New York,
NY 10016; (212) 532-6600

Produced by CLB Publishing
Godalming Business Centre
Woolsack Way, Godalming, Surrey, UK

ISBN 0-8317-7480-0

Printed in Hong Kong
10 9 8 7 6 5 4 3 2 1

PICTURE CREDITS
Photographs: 7 Allsport/David Cannon,
9 Phil Sheldon Photography, 10 Yours in Sport,
18(b) Allsport/David Cannon, 23 Yours in Sport,
29 Allsport/David Cannon, 32 Charles Briscoe-Knight,
52 Phil Sheldon Photography, 53 Allsport/David Cannon,
54 Phil Sheldon Photography, 55 Mark Newcombe,
58-59, 61(b) Phil Sheldon Photography,
65(b) Allsport/David Cannon
All other photographs: Eaglemoss/Phil Sheldon

Illustrations: Chris Perfect/ Egg Design

Cover: Centre left: Phil Sheldon Photography
Centre: Allsport/David Cannon
All others: Eaglemoss Publications

THE GOOD GOLF GUIDE

DRIVING FOR DISTANCE

SMITHMARK

CONTENTS

INTRODUCTION

It is every golfer's aim to hit a ball long and straight, but few players have the ability to achieve this with consistency. The search for length goes on and on. Is it my swing? Is it my club? Am I strong enough? Whatever the reason, you can now unravel the mysteries in your quest for a longer drive.

Driving for Distance takes an in-depth look at technique, the illustrations and text showing clearly how power is obtained. But achieving power can take a lot of hard work and dedication. First you must beat 'driver phobia' in order to gain those extra yards. Seek professional advice: go to your local professional, and with his help you can select the right club for your strength, thus saving you a lot of time and money.

How does Ian Woosnam hit so long? Why does Anders Forsbrand look so elegant? How can Sandy Lyle hit a 1 iron 260 yards? The answers to these questions and much more can be found within this book.

Driving the ball great distances gives more scope to Greg Norman's aggressive game. As he can easily reach par 5s in two shots, he can attack the pin for eagles.

USE YOUR WOODS FOR DISTANCE

What a difference a good tee shot makes. If you can strike the ball long and straight the game suddenly becomes easier. Firstly you must overcome the longer shaft and the desire to knock the cover off the ball, you will then be able to swing a wood like an iron and therefore attain a certain level of consistency. You need woods to gain those extra yards, so lets look at how to use them.

Although not one of the longest hitters in golf, Curtis Strange's consistently accurate driving is a hallmark of his game.

Using woods

You use the woods for maximum distance both on the tee and the fairway. Although woods are usually harder to control than irons, especially when you are new to the game, you should learn how to use them as soon as possible. Using woods to hit the ball long distances is an ability you must learn at an early stage to lower your scores.

A well-struck wood shot sets you up in the best possible way for the remainder of the hole.

The most commonly used woods are the 1, 3 and 5. They are designed to increase your distance and power without any extra effort.

While the size and shape of the clubhead provides the most obvious visual difference between woods and irons, it is the length of their shafts that helps you achieve the extra distance.

Shape, material and length combine with your technique to extract power from the club.

MORE POWER

When you swing a wood, the longer shaft gives a wider arc and this means that the clubhead has a greater distance to travel. If you swing a wood with the same rhythm and tempo as an iron, the clubhead travels around the arc in the same time, but it has to cover much more distance and this raises its speed. It is this increase in clubhead speed that provides you with the additional power to hit the ball longer dis-

WOOD AND IRON SWINGPLANES

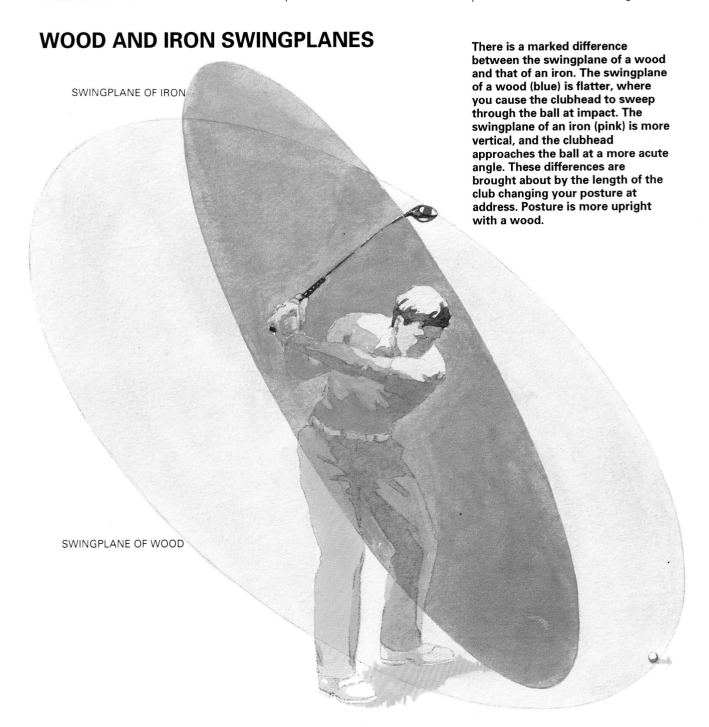

SWINGPLANE OF IRON

SWINGPLANE OF WOOD

There is a marked difference between the swingplane of a wood and that of an iron. The swingplane of a wood (blue) is flatter, where you cause the clubhead to sweep through the ball at impact. The swingplane of an iron (pink) is more vertical, and the clubhead approaches the ball at a more acute angle. These differences are brought about by the length of the club changing your posture at address. Posture is more upright with a wood.

SWINGING WITH WOODS

1 ADDRESS & TAKEAWAY
At address the ball is opposite the inside of your left heel. Take the club away slowly keeping the clubhead low to the ground.

2 ROTATE TO THE RIGHT
Allow your upper body to rotate freely as your left arm swings the club back. By the two-thirds point in your backswing your weight has transferred from a central position at address to the inside of your right foot.

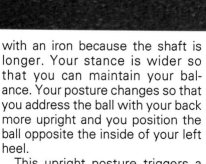

3 TOP OF THE BACKSWING
At the top of the backswing your shoulders have rotated 90° and your hips 45°. Make sure you complete the backswing before starting the downswing – a slight pause before the downswing helps. At the top of the backswing the shaft should point at the target.

tances. You do not have to speed up your swing and tempo to make the clubhead go faster. Your tempo should be the same for every 'full' shot from driving to pitching.

While the longer shaft of the wood should not affect your timing, it does lead to changes in your address including stance, posture and ball position. It also affects your swingplane.

ADDRESS AND SWINGPLANE

With a wood, you stand further away from the ball than you would with an iron because the shaft is longer. Your stance is wider so that you can maintain your balance. Your posture changes so that you address the ball with your back more upright and you position the ball opposite the inside of your left heel.

This upright posture triggers a number of other differences between woods and irons. Your swingplane is flatter, so the clubhead approaches the ball at a shallower angle. You sweep through the ball, which is struck at a later point in your swing. This is why the ball is placed opposite the inside of your left heel.

4 STARTING THE DOWNSWING
Rotate your left hip to the left to start the downswing. This pulls your arms and hands into an ideal striking position.

5 FOLLOWTHROUGH
After impact, allow your weight to move across to the outside of your left foot. The left side of your body controls the entire swing – from takeaway to followthrough – while your right side remains passive.

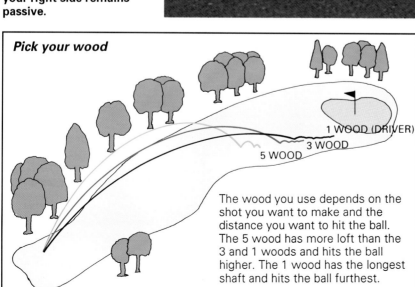

Pick your wood

1 WOOD (DRIVER)

3 WOOD

5 WOOD

The wood you use depends on the shot you want to make and the distance you want to hit the ball. The 5 wood has more loft than the 3 and 1 woods and hits the ball higher. The 1 wood has the longest shaft and hits the ball furthest.

6 THE COMPLETED POSITION
Allow the momentum of your club to pull your right shoulder and your head to face the target. Your whole body should also face the target. At the finish you should be balanced with most of your weight on your left foot.

BALL POSITION AT ADDRESS

FORWARD IN THE STANCE
With a wood, place the ball opposite the inside of your left heel and stand with your feet about as far apart as a normal walking pace is long. With a medium iron the ball is near the middle of your stance.

DISTANCE FROM FEET
Stand further away from the ball when you use a wood than you do with an iron. You have to do this because the shaft of a wood is longer.

THE BACKSWING

Once you have understood the changes to your stance, posture, ball position and swingplane, the basic technique for using woods is similar to using irons. Your tempo remains the same, as do your grip, aim and alignment procedures.

From address, take the club away slowly, keeping the clubhead close to the ground for the first 6-9in (15-23cm). Your left shoulder is pulled across and your weight

transfers from an even distribution at address to the inside of your right foot by the completion of the backswing.

PAUSE AT THE TOP

When you reach the top of your backswing, allow for a slight pause before starting the downswing. This pause helps create rhythm and improves timing by separating the backswing from the downswing. Many golfers believe that the backswing and downswing are one

continuous movement. This is wrong, and to treat them as one movement only leads to a rushed swing and a poor strike.

THE DOWNSWING

Begin the downswing by smoothly rotating your left hip to the left. This pulls your hands, arms and the clubhead down to the halfway position where your arms and hands swing the clubhead through the ball. The momentum of the clubhead pulls your right shoulder under your chin. Your head rotates to face the target and your weight moves across to your left foot.

TEEING UP THE BALL

When playing a wood shot from a tee peg you have to place the peg at the correct height. The height varies from club to club, but the general rule is that the centre of the ball should be level with the top of the clubface when the club is resting on the ground and the ball is on the tee.

Clubfaces on woods vary in depth, although within any one set, the lower the number of the wood then the deeper its clubface and bigger its clubhead. The 1 wood has the deepest clubface of all woods. The tee peg for a 1 wood should be higher than for a 3 wood, which in turn is higher than for a 5-wood. A ball teed at the correct height is easy to sweep off the top of the tee peg.

If you don't tee your ball at the correct height you lose both distance and accuracy or even mis-hit the shot.

TEEING HEIGHTS

When teeing up, half the ball should be above the top of the clubface at address. So, the deeper the clubface, the higher the tee peg should be set in the ground. Because the 1 wood has a deeper clubface than both the 3 and 5 wood, its tee peg should be

higher. The 5 wood has a shallower clubface so the ball is teed lower.

If you tee-up too high you might hit the ball with the top of the clubhead and send it into the sky. If you tee up too low you might hit the top of the ball and send it a short distance along the ground.

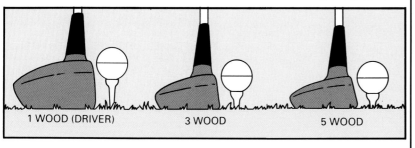

1 WOOD (DRIVER)   3 WOOD   5 WOOD

Practise your driving
It's vital to build a repeatable and consistent stroke with your woods. A long hit with your driver gives you the best possible chance of reaching the green of a long hole in few strokes. Practise with your woods until you are confident that you can hit long distances accurately. If you neglect any part of your game, the whole of your game is bound to suffer.

Increase your distance

Everyone has the potential to hit the ball further. You can do it simply by increasing your clubhead speed through impact with the ball. Brute force, however, is not the answer – trying to hit it as hard as possible usually results in completely missing your target.

To increase the distance in your game – and also improve your accuracy – you need to consider carefully certain aspects of your swing.

The four keys are: relaxing at address to eliminate stress; keeping your left arm extended; transferring your weight correctly to hit through the ball; and perfecting your tempo – the timing and rhythm of your swing.

RELAX AT ADDRESS

When thinking about distance, the automatic reaction is to tense up before hitting the shot. But this destroys your ability to move freely and correctly – so you lose distance and accuracy.

The feeling throughout your body should be one of calm anticipation,

IMPACT
For an accurate, long-hitting shot, every aspect of your swing must be correct.

SHOULDERS
Your shoulders must rotate correctly, working together with the left arm to form the arc for an effective golf swing.

GRIP
Stay relaxed. Gripping too tightly makes your body go rigid, as well as locking away any chance of achieving extra distance.

KNEES
Locking your knees at any stage of the swing has a disastrous effect on your ability to move. Your knees must stay 'soft'.

CLUBFACE
The clubface must be square as you hit through, not at, the ball. Good distance is worthless without accuracy.

HITTING THROUGH THE BALL

1 STARTING THE BACKSWING
Keep a relaxed grip on the club at address and then start the swing with a slow takeaway. This lets your weight begin its movement easily across to your right side.

2 SHOULDER MOVEMENT
With the club halfway back, your shoulders rotate through nearly a quarter turn – almost 90°. This starts the shift of weight to the right foot.

3 COILING YOUR POWER
Your weight moves to the inside of your right foot and your right knee remains flexed. Your left heel lifts slightly to let the left side of your body rotate.

5 IMPACT POSITION
The left side of your body is in control, with the weight moving across to your left foot. The lightness in your hands at address lets the club square itself naturally. This does not happen if you are tense.

6 HEAD POSITION
Let your head rotate as you begin followthrough. Do not keep it down too long as this hinders followthrough. Your body must follow the club so that its momentum pulls your right side through.

rather like the sprinter in the blocks. Although motionless, he has to remain relaxed if he is to make a smooth and sharp start to the run.

Tension often begins in the grip. A grip that is too tight causes the muscles in your forearms to lock up. This locking of muscles travels upwards through your arms and into your shoulders. You must make sure that you keep a secure grip without clutching the club too hard. If you feel you are gripping too tightly, release your hold and start again.

The lower body is the foundation of the swing, so it has to work freely and naturally. Try to keep your knees 'soft' while preparing to swing the club.

EXTENDED LEFT ARM

The movement of your left arm, combined with the rotation of your shoulders, forms the arc of the golf swing. It produces the clubhead

speed required to propel the ball. One way to maximize your distance is to make sure that your left arm is behaving properly during the swing. If your left arm bends in the backswing, it reduces the width of the arc, causing loss of clubhead speed.

At address, your left arm should hang straight, but not rigid. When beginning the backswing, you should feel your left arm and shoulder move in unison to keep the left side extension. At the top of the backswing, your left arm should be as it was at address.

As the downswing begins, your left hip moves smoothly out of the way to let your left arm and body swing through. Your left arm stays extended throughout this movement. At impact, it should still be in the same position it was in at address. It is only after impact, as the club moves through, that your arm gradually folds at the elbow for the followthrough and completion of the swing.

4 STORING YOUR POWER
Begin the downswing by turning your left hip. This starts the weight shift to your left side, and pulls your arms, hands and club down.

7 FOLLOWING THROUGH
Allow your weight to transfer to the outside of your left foot, letting your left knee stay flexed. Your head now rotates upwards. Only a little weight remains on the right toe.

8 COMPLETION
Your entire body rotates to face the target, pulled by the momentum of the clubhead. Throughout the swing, maintain your balance and keep the rhythm smooth.

WEIGHT TRANSFER

A powerful golf swing relies on correct weight transfer.

As the backswing and body rotation begin, let your weight move across easily to the inside of the right foot. The weight transfer co-ordinates with the rotation of the body.

At the top of the backswing, almost 90% of your body weight has transferred to the inside of your right foot. Your shoulders have rotated 90° and your hips 45°. You must maintain your balance, with no weight moving to the outside of your right foot.

The downswing begins from your left hip, which moves smoothly to the left. This automatically transfers your weight to the left foot and pulls the club down, so that it is ready to hit through the ball. Your arms and hands release the full power of the clubhead into the back of the ball. The momentum of the clubhead now pulls the right side of your body under and through.

STRAIGHT LEFT ARM
Your left arm forms the arc of a powerful swing, so it should stay fairly straight but relaxed in the backswing (1). Extending your left side (2) gives the swing consistency and power. At impact (3), both arms are in almost exactly the same position as at address. Control from the left side helps you to swing through the ball, not across it – and increases power.

Greg Norman – distance master
One of the most powerful hitters on the professional scene is the Australian, Greg Norman. He hits the ball huge distances with almost every club in the bag.

Norman does not place his club on the ground at address. He holds it above the ground to help a smooth, slow, deliberate takeaway (start of the backswing). As the club reaches the top of the backswing, there is almost a pause before Norman's immense power is uncoiled into and through the golf ball. The ball starts its flight low and rises slowly but surely before falling to earth again, usually a massive 270yd (245m) along the fairway.

Norman uses his power to crush opponents, reaching par 5 holes with a drive and a medium iron. He even reaches some par 4 holes in one stroke.

TEMPO

A good, even tempo is essential for maximum distance. Weight transfer and a wide, full swing motion need time to work well.

A wild thrash at the ball leaves little time to store and then release the power required for an effective throughswing. A lot depends on a slow, unhurried backswing. This is characteristic of many long hitters. As the downswing begins, the power is gradually released through the ball.

pro tip

What's in a name?
One way of improving your tempo is to say 'Severiano Ballesteros'. The 'Severiano' is said on the backswing and the 'Ballesteros' on the down and throughswing: the 'Balle' is the start of the downswing, the 'ster' coincides with impact and the 'os' is the followthrough. The Spanish star's name is such a mouthful that it corrects your timing.

Tempo and rhythm

To be a consistent striker of the ball your swing must have good tempo and rhythm. Tempo is the speed at which you swing the club while rhythm is its fluency.

Good tempo and rhythm allow every moving part of your body to co-ordinate as a single unit. Although your head, shoulders, arms, hands, hips, knees and feet have their own function, they must work together during the swing. If your tempo is too fast or erratic, this doesn't happen and you don't make a solid strike.

Even if your set-up is perfect and you swing the clubhead along the correct path, you only play effective golf when your tempo and rhythm are relaxed and smooth.

DEVELOPING YOUR TEMPO

Most players with poor tempo and rhythm swing the club too fast in a vain attempt to work up power and distance. A quick or rushed swing doesn't allow each individual movement enough time to perform its task and your action is jerky.

To find your natural tempo and rhythm concentrate on swinging the club smoothly. Start with a half swing. Only when you achieve a solid, consistent strike should you lengthen your swing to three-quarter and then full.

Developing your ideal tempo and rhythm takes practice as well as natural ability. Once they improve you can build a repeatable swing.

It is vital you concentrate on keeping a good tempo and rhythm when playing a round. Once you've

SWINGING SMOOTHLY
Good tempo and rhythm allow each individual movement within your swing to work correctly and help produce a perfect swing path. If your swing is too quick your body hasn't enough time to rotate properly and the clubface isn't square at impact.

UNDERSTANDING TEMPO AND RHYTHM

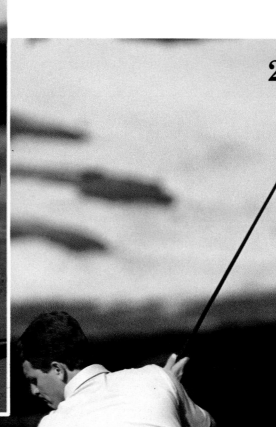

1

2

1　TAKEAWAY
The takeaway dictates the speed of the swing. If you rush it, the rest of your swing becomes too fast and erratic. Concentrate on taking the club away smoothly.

2　THE BACKSWING
Your backswing must have a smooth and even rhythm. This allows your hands, arms and shoulders to move as one, and helps you to feel the clubhead throughout the stroke.

3　TOP OF BACKSWING
Allow for a slight pause at the top of the backswing to ensure that you complete it. This prevents you from rushing the downswing.

selected the club to fit into your game plan, your only thought should be making a smooth swing. Visualize your swing as a whole. Avoid analysing any specific movement within your swing just as you blot out hazards on the fairway.

RECOVERING LOST TEMPO

No player – even leading professionals – consistently maintains perfect tempo and rhythm. Regaining your timing isn't difficult – as long as you go back to basics.

Once you establish a regular distance with each club, recover lost tempo and rhythm by playing to a shorter target. Reduce the distance you try to send each shot by about one-third. This automatically slows your swing down, allowing each body movement enough time to function.

By slowing down and reducing the length of your swing you lessen

4 THE DOWNSWING
The downswing must have the same tempo and swing path as the backswing. To help you swing the club on the same line, the start of the downswing must be smooth.

5 IMPACT
To make a solid strike your tempo and rhythm must be perfect. Your swing movements must co-ordinate properly so that the clubface is square at impact.

6 FOLLOWTHROUGH
Your swing slows down as smoothly as it increased at takeaway. Good tempo and rhythm look effortless and should become natural and consistent with regular practice.

SHORTEN YOUR SWING

One of the best ways to improve – as well as understand – tempo and rhythm is to practise a three-quarter swing. By shortening your swing you slow it down and it is easier for its individual movements to co-ordinate correctly. A three-quarter swing also increases clubhead feel.

tension and develop greater clubhead feel. You also hit the ball further than you expect because you achieve a more solid strike.

With a slower action it is easier to identify any faults in your set-up and swing – and then correct them. From here you can increase your tempo until your swing combines rhythm, consistency and power.

FEET TOGETHER

Another exercise for finding good tempo and rhythm is to hit the ball with your feet together. Because your centre of gravity is higher than with a normal stance you must reduce the speed, length and power of your swing to avoid losing balance.

The best way to understand and appreciate tempo and rhythm is to watch top players – either at tournaments or on television. Although they all swing the club differently their tempo and rhythm are perfect.

Take an image of their swing on to the practice range or course and try to copy it. It's amazing how you can improve your own swing – and your game – by trying to imitate top players.

REDUCE YOUR DISTANCE

If your swing is too fast, slow it down by reducing the distance you try to hit each shot. For example, if you normally expect to strike a 5 iron about 150yd (136m), go to the practice ground and aim at a target 100yd (91m) away. This makes you reduce the length, speed and power of your normal swing, and helps you develop a smoother action.

FAIRWAY WOODS

When you require distance a wood is far easier to hit than a long iron. Try a 5 wood then move on to a 3 wood – you'll soon see that the woods really do work. Faced with anything from 160 yards to 200 yards in the light semi-rough try your 5 wood instead of a long iron; a wood will sweep through the grass whereas an iron tends to dig in. When you get really confident you can try the driver off the fairway.

Ray Floyd uses his legs to generate power, as demonstrated in this shot from the 1987 USPGA.

Fairway woods

Fairway woods – used for distance – are commonly referred to as numbers 2, 3, 4 and 5. Most players carry two – usually a 3 and 5.

There are similarities between a fairway wood and a driver (1 wood). Both hit the ball a long way. The clubhead on both is made from wood, metal or graphite. But fair-

way woods are designed to hit the ball off the ground and are ideal for your second shot on long par 4s and par 5s.

The clubhead on a fairway wood has a low centre of gravity so that most of its weight hits below the middle of the ball, which helps to propel it upwards.

This is not the case with a driver,

MAXIMUM FAIRWAY DISTANCE
If you need top distance from the fairway take a wood. It is easier to use than a long iron because of its bigger clubface loft and rounded clubhead – which sweeps through impact more smoothly than an iron.

SWINGING A FAIRWAY WOOD

1 ADDRESS POSITION
At address the ball is opposite the inside of your left heel and your posture is more upright than normal.

2 MID BACKSWING
Rotate your upper body to the right, keeping the clubhead close to the ground for the first 6-9in (15-22cm). Your left arm remains straight for the takeaway.

3 TOP OF BACKSWING
At the top of the backswing your upper body has rotated halfway – about 90° – and your lower body about 45°. The club's shaft points at the target.

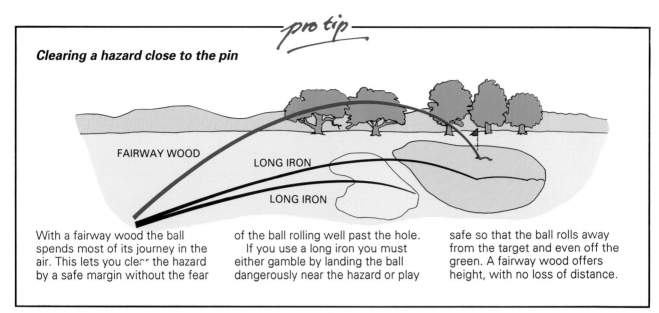

pro tip

Clearing a hazard close to the pin

FAIRWAY WOOD

LONG IRON

LONG IRON

With a fairway wood the ball spends most of its journey in the air. This lets you clear the hazard by a safe margin without the fear of the ball rolling well past the hole.

If you use a long iron you must either gamble by landing the ball dangerously near the hazard or play safe so that the ball rolls away from the target and even off the green. A fairway wood offers height, with no loss of distance.

4   THE DOWNSWING
On the downswing your body starts to uncoil, led by your left hip which rotates to the left. The downswing must be smooth and unhurried.

5   THROUGH IMPACT
The clubhead is swept through the ball by power generated on the downswing. Don't let your head lift up too early on the followthrough.

6   FINAL POSITION
At the end of the swing your upper body and head face the target, with most of your weight on your left foot. Your finish should be balanced and relaxed.

which has a clubhead with a high centre of gravity and is designed to play a raised ball from a tee peg. Don't take a driver from the fairway because most of its weight is above the centre of the ball.

EASY TO USE

The 3 and 5 woods hit the ball about the same distance as the 1 and 2 irons. When faced with a long shot, the high handicap player should choose a wood.

A fairway wood gives much better height than an iron – it has a lower centre of gravity and a bigger clubface loft. The rounded clubhead also sweeps through impact more smoothly than a long iron, especially in the rough.

While long irons give slightly more control when struck perfectly, they are so difficult to use that only low handicap golfers and professionals are skilful enough to play with them. An average player achieves a consistently better strike with a fairway wood.

HEIGHT AND LENGTH

A fairway wood is one of the most versatile clubs in your bag, combining height with length. Not only does it hit the ball as far as a long iron, it also hits it higher.

If your path is blocked by a tall obstacle, such as a tree, hedge or wall, a fairway wood often provides quick enough lift for your ball

The fairway woods

2 WOOD **3 WOOD** **4 WOOD** **5 WOOD**

There are four fairway woods – a 2, 3, 4 and 5 – although most players carry only a 3 and 5 wood. The lower the number, the steeper the clubface and bigger the clubhead. Low numbers give you most distance; high numbers give you most height.

to clear any problems. A long iron is unlikely to give you a successful shot.

PLAYING THE SHOT

Grip the club normally and stand with the ball opposite the inside of your left heel. Aim the clubface square to the target and align your body parallel to the ball-to-target line. Make sure that the sole of the clubhead rests flat on the ground at address.

Because of the long shaft, your posture is more upright than normal. This creates a flat swing plane. Take the club away slowly, keeping a smooth tempo during the entire swing. The clubface sweeps the ball cleanly off the turf without taking a divot.

Remember you don't have to increase the speed of your swing to find extra distance. Power and clubhead speed are created by the long shaft, which in turn produces a wider arc.

Do's and don'ts
- DO use a 2, 3, 4 or 5 wood for distance from fairway or rough, and for height to clear an obstacle.
- DO check that the ball is opposite the inside of your left heel, and further away from your feet than for an iron to allow for the longer shaft.
- DO keep an even tempo.
- DON'T increase the speed of your swing.
- DON'T use a driver from the fairway.
- DON'T take a gamble – in a tricky lie choose your most lofted wood.

Which wood?

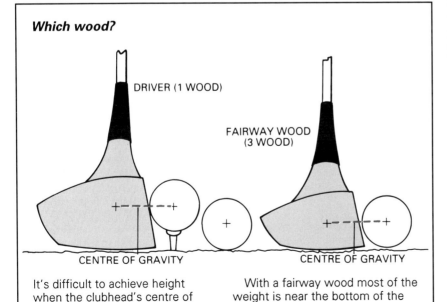

DRIVER (1 WOOD)

FAIRWAY WOOD (3 WOOD)

CENTRE OF GRAVITY

CENTRE OF GRAVITY

It's difficult to achieve height when the clubhead's centre of gravity is above the middle of the ball at impact. A driver has a high centre of gravity and is designed for striking a ball off a tee peg.

With a fairway wood most of the weight is near the bottom of the clubhead. It strikes below the centre of a ball on the ground, propelling it upwards without sacrificing distance.

Driver off the fairway

The driver off the fairway is an extremely effective weapon when used in the correct way. But it should only be played when you can gain a definite advantage.

The shot produces a low-boring trajectory – ideal when hitting into wind, or for a long running ball to a distant target – but it's also difficult to play perfectly. Only advanced players should attempt this shot – it's not for high handicappers.

WEIGH UP THE RISKS

Use the shot to reach a long par 4 into the wind or to get home in 2 on a par 5. Yet if there is only a small chance of success and trouble looms near the green, it's wiser to play a long iron and then

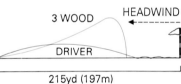

Short for control
When confronted by a shot into wind of roughly 3 wood distance, it's sometimes better to go down the grip on your driver and shorten your backswing.

The three-quarter backswing means the ball doesn't go as far as a normal driver but you have more control over the shot. The ball flies low and runs towards the target, while a full 3 wood shot is more affected by the wind as the ball climbs higher than with a driver.

You may be pleasantly surprised how far the ball goes using this method, especially on a firm, dry fairway.

3 WOOD   HEADWIND

DRIVER

215yd (197m)

THOUGHT AND TEMPO
The secret of success is positive and careful thinking, while maintaining good rhythm with a normal swing. With the feet slightly open the ball starts fractionally left and slides back to the right during flight. The ball flies low and can run long distances, perfect for playing into wind.

hit a short iron in.

The lie must be flat or slightly uphill – to act as a launching pad – and the ball must be sitting well, preferably on dry ground. When the ball is lying badly always think hard about hitting the shot even if there is a chance of reaching the green. It's a tricky enough shot to play well without added problems.

Many regard the driver off the fairway as the hardest of all shots, but as long as the lie is good the risks are mainly in the mind.

The fact that most good golfers happily hit a 3 wood off the fairway makes their fear all the more unnecessary.

There is only a slight difference in the degree of loft, the centre of gravity and length of shaft from a 3 wood to a driver. The driver is just a bit more difficult to play.

THE TECHNIQUE

The basic technique of hitting the driver from the fairway is the same as from a tee peg. At address, position the ball opposite or slightly in front of your left heel and aim the clubface at the target as normal.

Your feet should be fractionally open – this slightly increases the loft on the driver to help get the ball airborne and to guard against the snap hook. Because you are aligning slightly left and your clubface is square, the ball starts left and moves gently to the right in the flight.

Think positively – imagine you are hitting a 3 wood – and swing as normal. Don't overhit the ball – rhythm is far more important when applying power.

The key difference between hitting off the fairway and from a tee peg is timing. It needs to be spot on to achieve good results from the fairway. It's important to strike the ball at the bottom of your swing arc, and to sweep it off the turf.

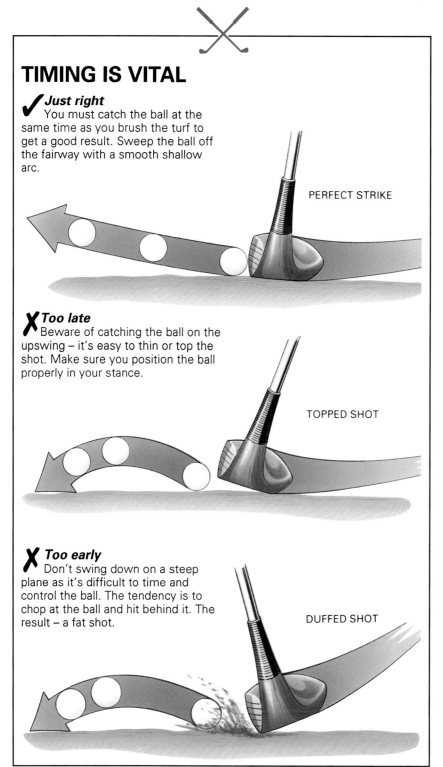

TIMING IS VITAL

✓ Just right
You must catch the ball at the same time as you brush the turf to get a good result. Sweep the ball off the fairway with a smooth shallow arc.

PERFECT STRIKE

✗ Too late
Beware of catching the ball on the upswing – it's easy to thin or top the shot. Make sure you position the ball properly in your stance.

TOPPED SHOT

✗ Too early
Don't swing down on a steep plane as it's difficult to time and control the ball. The tendency is to chop at the ball and hit behind it. The result – a fat shot.

DUFFED SHOT

masterclass

Ian's killer blow
The driver from the fairway presents Ian Woosnam with few problems because he is such a great timer of the ball. Combined with his power he can reach greens that are out of range for most golfers.

In the 1989 Irish Open at Portmarnock, the little Welshman came to the 514yd par-5 16th neck and neck with Philip Walton. But Woosie struck two drivers one after the other – the second off the fairway – to within 15ft (5m) of the hole to make birdie. He went on to win the title.

Lanny Wadkins: king of the fairway wood

F orget about the armchair pundits, when your fellow pros vote you the best fairway wood player on tour it really means you're the best. That is exactly what the US Tour golfers have said about the seven time Ryder Cup star Lanny Wadkins for years.

Renowned for his no-nonsense approach and magical matchplay abilities, no opponent can ever take Lanny for granted. No one can afford to be complacent after finding the green from long range, if Wadkins is 230yd (210m) away with his 4 wood in hand. He can lay one in there with ease and leave them scrambling for a half.

SWISH HITTER

His fast-hitting, attacking style wins many admirers, but the flurry of wood and steel is not just an aggressive swipe – there is method in his action. The 'fastest gun in the west' – a nickname coined because of his speedy approach to the game – is slightly unorthodox, but bases his superb hitting on sound fundamentals.

Lanny's shot visualization and striking are the most impressive parts of his fairway wood play, and every golfer can learn from his method.

By subtly changing his set-up and swing the burly Virginian manufactures exquisite strokes. Whether it's a low, drilling wind cheater or a high, soft-landing floater, Lanny knows the exact technique needed to bring it off.

He takes time to weigh up the stroke, thinking of the shape of shot he needs and the set-up and swing to produce it. But after careful thought he is quick to get into position and fire the ball away – he never dwells.

GET SET UP, GO

As long as you visualize the shot carefully before you play, there is no need to take time over the stroke. Like Lanny, walk into position, set up and then go for it. If your swing thoughts are correct for the shape of shot you need, only doubts can creep in if you loiter over the ball.

But striking the ball quite quickly after setting up doesn't mean you have to swing fast as well. Though Lanny has a quick tempo, his rhythm is good and he keeps himself under control throughout the swing.

POWER FADE PERFECTION

1 SMART SET-UP
Once decided on hitting his stock fairway wood shot – the high power fade – Wadkins moves quickly into position. With the blade square to the target and his feet, hips and shoulders slightly open, Lanny looks relaxed and ready to go.

2 POWER EXTENSION
The extension on the takeaway is enormous. His left arm is still perfectly straight, and this creates a very wide swing arc. His legs are active and he has already turned his shoulders a good deal. All of Lanny's backswing moves are designed to produce power.

3 TOP MODEL
A powerful action is no good unless your club swings on line. Lanny completes his massive shoulder-turning backswing on perfect plane. There is no hint of an arched or cupped left wrist, which means the clubface is square at the top. If you move into a coiled position like Lanny's, you have a great base to swing down into impact on the correct path.

4 DYNAMICALLY DOWN
From the top, Lanny drops his hands down forcefully towards the ball leaving his clubhead trailing way behind. Instead of flailing his arms uncontrollably to the outside – as many amateurs do when they swing aggressively – he controls the slight out-to-in path by keeping his right arm tucked in.

5 EXACTING STRIKE
Fast hands enable Lanny to return the blade square. Combined with an excellent drive of his legs into and through impact they create a huge amount of power. His balance and clubhead control are so good throughout the swing that he strikes the ball sweetly and true. A full release of the hands through impact is also essential for control.

6 FLOWING AND STABLE
Lanny stays superbly balanced on his full and flowing throughswing. Staying with the shot – keeping the head behind the ball through impact – ensures that all the good moves on the backswing and downswing aren't wasted by rising off the shot.

7 HIGH HANDS, HIGH BALL
Because Lanny maintains a good rhythm, strikes fractionally down on the shot and swings on a slightly out-to-in path, the ball starts a fraction left of target and rises high. These traits are all essential to hit a controlled, left-to-right, soft-landing wood.

IMPROVE YOUR SWING

To obtain power and accuracy you must develop a consistent and rhythmical swing. To do this you will need to work on all parts of your swing, whether it be the backswing, downswing, impact or follow-through. Power is a combination of co-ordinated body movements. Learn to use your weight correctly and perfect your balance.

**Sam Torrance shows his style at
the 1989 English Open.**

Create good body turn

Full body rotation is vital to a powerful and accurate golf swing. If you want to increase the distance you hit your shots and use the clubs to their potential, you must turn smoothly and competently on both your back-swing and throughswing.

You achieve good body turn by starting your backswing with your whole left side. Make sure that you don't fall into the most common trap – swinging with your hands and arms only.

TURN YOUR SHOULDERS

The takeaway begins with your left side rotating towards the right. This continues until the top of the

THE NEED FOR A FULL TURN
Proper body turn is the key to a powerful swing along the correct plane. Rotating your shoulders fully means that you use all your strength to gain maximum distance and helps to ensure an accurate, clean strike. Less supple players can lift their left heel slightly to help them turn on the backswing.

TRAIN YOURSELF TO TURN FULLY

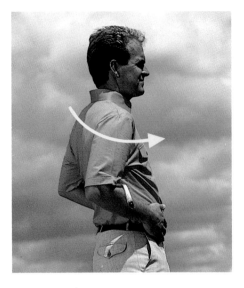

1 **Practise making a full turn –** both back and through. Begin by holding an iron club halfway up your back and flexing your knees.

2 **Slide your left side smoothly** round to the right so that your shoulders are at right angles to your starting position.

3 **Swivel back fully to the left.** Your shoulders are again 90° to your starting point – though facing in the opposite direction.

USING YOUR WHOLE LEFT SIDE

1 **PLACE AN EXTRA BALL**
With one ball in its normal position, place another about 18in (45cm) behind it, a couple of ball widths closer to your feet. The balls are not level because you want to encourage a correct plane. Set up parallel, as normal – use a spare club for correct alignment.

2 **SWEEP THE SECOND BALL**
As your left side starts to slide right on the takeaway, the back of the clubhead sweeps away the second ball. If the clubhead passes above, inside or outside the second ball, you're swinging too much with your hands and arms.

backswing, when your left side begins its journey back. It pulls your arms and hands down – they're now loaded with power – and you release the clubhead at impact with force and accuracy.

Body turn does not end at impact. As your hands and arms swing the club through, your upper body keeps turning. Only at the top of the followthrough should your shoulders finally catch up with your hips.

All these movements must work together to form a complete, slick swing. Your body must find the key positions if you're to become consistent.

ELASTIC TENSION

As you start the backswing, your arms and hands – the only part of your body in contact with the club – move because your shoulders do. Your left knee and right hip respond.

Your back must face the target at the top of the backswing and your left arm should be straight.

You need to create lively tension in your leg and back muscles to store maximum power at the top of the backswing – as if you're stretching an elastic band. The only way to achieve elastic tension is by turning your shoulders 90° and your hips 45°.

STRAIGHT LEFT ARM

Many players fail to complete their shoulder turn because they don't feel they can return the club smoothly to impact. They stop their shoulder turn halfway and complete the backswing by breaking the left arm. When this happens you lose all control and power.

Turning your hips as far as your shoulders also causes problems. You lose all tension – and store no power.

The positive tension at the top of the backswing unwinds during the downswing. Your upper body pulls your arms and hands to the downswing's mid point. They're loaded with power and about to release at exactly the right time – impact.

CLUBHEAD SPEED

The more tension you create between your hips and shoulders the more clubhead speed you produce – which increases distance.

Let clubhead speed help bring your right shoulder round to the left after impact. The shoulder in turn forces your head up to watch the ball as you swivel round to a full finish.

FULL SHOULDER TURN
At the top of the backswing your shoulders have correctly turned 90° and your hips 45°. To hit the second ball, you had to start your takeaway by moving your hips, shoulders, hands and arms together.

pro tip

LEFT SHOULDER OVER RIGHT INSTEP

Look at your left shoulder
As you hold the club at the top, look down at your left shoulder, which should be directly in your field of view. You've turned well if it fills the space just inside your right foot.

Improve the downswing

The aim of the downswing is to return the clubface square to the ball with as much power as you can deliver – you need good tempo and rhythm to maintain the flow.

The downswing is the most complex movement to learn and perfect. You are usually taught the backswing and downswing as two separate parts, but in fact the downswing begins before the backswing has ended. They must now be put together to form one fluent movement.

Your backswing prepares you to strike the ball. In completing it, the upper body coils 90° while the lower body turns only 45°. The lower body becomes the trigger for your downswing. Your weight has shifted to your right hip pocket area and you should be in a relaxed and powerful position.

THE TRIGGER

The key to making a good downswing is to link your legs to your arms correctly. Your chest, arms, wrists and hands must move together.

If you raise your left heel during the backswing, the downswing begins by you firmly planting it back on the ground. This action triggers the left hip and starts a weight shift back to the left side.

If you are young and supple you don't need to lift your left heel to complete the backswing. The left hip now starts the downswing, pulling the hands, arms and club down to the mid point position.

POWER AND ACCURACY

This movement automatically drops the club on a path slightly inside that of your backswing. Any sudden or awkward move at this

STARTING THE DOWNSWING
The downswing begins before the backswing has ended – your hips start to move back to the ball before you reach the top point.

YOUR HEAD
Although your left eye should be looking down on the back of the ball, your head has turned slightly to the right.

UPPER BODY
Turn your chest so that your back faces the target. Your upper body rotates 90° from the address position.

LEGS AND LOWER BODY
Your legs are flexed and ready to provide power through the ball. They turn only 45°.

PERFECTING THE DOWNSWING

pro tip

Turn into impact
To imitate the position your body should be in at impact, adopt your normal address position with your hands and arms stretched out. Concentrate on turning your left hip to the left which twists your middle body towards the target. Do this slowly four or five times so you can see how correct hip rotation returns the arms to impact.

1 THE TOP
At the top point you should feel poised and ready for action. Your upper body coils 90° while your hips turn 45° and provide stability for your swing. Feel your weight transfer to your right hip pocket. The right knee remains flexed to let the legs support the upper body. The shaft of the club should point parallel to your ball-to-target line.

2 FIRST MOVEMENT
Turn your left hip smoothly to the left. This triggers the weight shift back to your left side. Feel your left hip linked to your left hand and arm – they all move together and must not separate. As the left hip starts the downswing, the hands and arms automatically drop inside the path of the backswing. This natural movement starts before you've completed the backswing.

3 MID POINT
The hands and arms respond to the movement of your lower body. The hips continue to lower the hands and arms towards the ball. This is where you should feel immensely powerful. But don't attempt to hit the ball at this stage – your power is stored in your wrists, which must not unhinge too early in the swing.

4 READY FOR IMPACT
As you continue to turn the left hip to the left, the clubhead returns back to the ball and is naturally square at impact. Using your hips and legs correctly means no conscious hand action is necessary.

point is disastrous. At the mid point, your left arm acts as a powerful lever, pulling the clubhead into the ball and storing power.

Your hands and arms are responding to the movement of your lower body. As the left hip continues turning to the left the hands and arms deliver the clubhead back to the ball with power and accuracy.

WEIGHT TRANSFER

During the downswing your weight transfers from your right side to your left – by impact slightly more than half your weight is on the inside of your left foot. Your head stays still until you strike the ball.

You must feel the downswing with your feet. They help generate power and co-ordinate the entire swing. If the hip and leg action is incorrect you lose all smoothness. Correct hip rotation allows your arms, wrists and hands to remain passive.

If your lower body doesn't rotate correctly on the downswing, your hands, wrists and arms shape the swing path. The clubhead moves outside the ball-to-target line at the start of the downswing before being pulled across your body from out to in. At impact the clubface isn't square and you slice the ball.

Improve your followthrough

Your followthrough – sometimes called the throughswing – is vital to your swing. You must swing through to a good finish on all your shots – this promotes accuracy and power and helps you keep smooth rhythm and tempo.

Unfortunately many golfers concentrate so hard on hitting the ball that they forget about achieving a correct followthrough. They quit on the ball and lose power and distance. Your swing does not finish when you hit the ball – the golf swing is complete when your body turns round to a balanced finish after impact.

The finish provides a good guide to the rest of your swing as it confirms the movements you have made before. Look for clues in your

pro tip

Hold your finish
To help you create a positive, firm followthrough, stay in your finished position until the ball either reaches the top of its flight or lands. This encourages you to make a complete swing. Don't feel that you've done all the work when you hit the ball.

COMPLETE YOUR SWING

A solid followthrough is an essential part of the complete golf swing. A repeatable swing is your goal so to perfect your movements you must assume the key positions consistently.

HEAD FORCED UP
Your head is forced up as your right shoulder comes round. This lets your arms swing the club around your body to the finish.

WEIGHT TRANSFER
After impact your body must keep turning – and your weight should transfer – to the left. As this happens your right shoulder swivels in the same direction.

CLUBHEAD SPEED
At a point just after impact the clubhead reaches top speed. It is this speed – with proper weight transfer – that carries you through to the followthrough position.

BALANCE
You finish steady on your feet – most of the weight is on the outside of your left foot, with your right foot almost vertical.

Trouble both sides

When you're playing a tough hole with trouble on both sides, your confidence is likely to waver – just when you need it most.

Lack of confidence in the throughswing causes you to quit on the shot after impact. Without a proper throughswing your strike is stifled and balance impaired. You need to know that you can rely on repeating your finish position, so that you play a powerful – and straight – stroke, even under pressure.

Concentrate on your followthrough – that's when the shot finishes, not when you hit the ball. Thinking about your finish helps take your mind off any pressure – and off impact – so that you focus on rhythm throughout your swing.

followthrough to diagnose swing faults.

REVERSE THE BACKSWING

Most players realize that good body turn is vital during the backswing – but forget that they need to repeat this on the followthrough.

To help build your through-swing, you can reverse an exercise you tried when you were developing the backswing.

Set yourself into your final followthrough position and rewind your body, arms and club until you come back to the impact position. This helps you to find the correct throughswing plane – it should feel like your backswing reversed.

It's unlikely that you'll achieve a valid followthrough unless your top of the backswing position is good.

Tempo is vital – it gives each part of your body the time to respond correctly and evenly during the swing. Smooth rhythm leads to a regular, clean strike as the moving parts of your body slot into the proper places. You must have fluid movement from the top of the backswing to the end of the throughswing to promote this tempo either side of impact.

WEIGHT TRANSFER

A good followthrough needs sound weight transfer. From the top of the backswing – when most of your weight is on the right foot – you shift your weight to the left. In your finish position you should be balanced with most of your weight on the outside of your left foot.

If you don't shift your weight properly you're likely to stay flat footed as you swing through, and

MAKING A CLASSIC FOLLOWTHROUGH

1 INTO IMPACT
Your hips lead your shoulders all the way on the downswing as you make a smooth strike through the ball. At impact you're just beginning to lift your right heel up.

2 FLUID MOVEMENT
Keep your movements smooth after you strike – just because you've hit the ball, it doesn't mean that you've finished playing the shot. Your head remains still.

A MATTER OF BALANCE

✓ A sound throughswing means that you're steady, with most weight on the outside of your left foot. The ball gains good distance.

✗ If your weight fails to shift from right to left on the downswing, you're left flat footed. In most cases this leads to a slice.

✗ Throwing your lower body weight too much right to left on the downswing leaves you likely to overbalance forwards. It usually causes a push.

3 HEAD COMES ROUND

Your upper body continues to clear to the left, so that your turning right shoulder begins to force your head round and up to watch the ball's flight. Most of your weight has shifted to the left side.

4 SHOULDERS CATCH UP

Because your head has come round, your upper body clearance is not obstructed, helping you apply maximum power. Your shoulders catch up with your hips at the end of the swing. Your right foot is vertical, resting lightly on the ground.

WHERE ARE YOU FACING?

1 BACKSWING
Use a club to check your position. A good backswing leads to an effective throughswing. At the top of your backswing, your followthrough is reversed – your shoulders are 90° to the ball-to-target line. Your back faces the target and the club is almost horizontal.

2 DOWNSWING
The smooth tempo on your downswing should be the same as on your throughswing – the club must not slow down. By impact, your rotating upper body should be parallel to the ball-to-target line.

3 THROUGHSWING
Your finish is like the top of the backswing reversed. Your shoulders are 90° to the ball-to-target line, and your chest faces the target.

you lose distance. This usually happens because you start the downswing with your hands and arms instead of working from your hips. You don't have time to transfer weight before impact.

Pushing too hard with your lower body also causes erratic weight transfer. You fail to swing around your body, making a balanced finish impossible.

HEAD MOVEMENT

Keeping your head down too long after impact destroys any chance you had of achieving a correct followthrough.

Watch the clubhead strike the ball but then let your right shoulder – which should be turning smoothly left – gently force your head round to face the target. If your head stays down too long it gets in the way of your body's clearing action and prevents a full followthrough.

Complete your lower body turn

✗ The lower body must be correct if the upper body is to follow suit. Bringing your legs and hips only part of the way round reduces your chances of making a full, powerful strike.

✓ Your throughswing is fully effective only if your lower body completes its turn, and you end in a balanced position with your weight mainly on the outside of your left foot.

Weight transfer

There's more than one way to strike a golf ball well, but if you want to hit good shots on a regular basis you must transfer your weight correctly during the swing. With a good weight shift power flows smoothly from your body through to the club and the ball.

For a full shot, a little more than half your weight should be on your right foot at the top of the backswing. As you start the down-swing your weight gradually shifts towards the target. And when you complete your followthrough, you must have almost all of your weight on your left foot.

You may get away with a less than classical action. Many great players in the past have prospered with an unorthodox swing – Arnold Palmer and Lee Trevino are two perfect examples. But correct weight transfer is an essential ingredient of every successful golf swing – once you've got it right, don't tamper with it.

ADDRESSING THE PROBLEM

Take the first steps to correct weight transfer before you swing the club. At address make sure your weight is equally distributed on both feet. It's much easier to build a good swing if the foundations are solid.

Any fault is likely to cause you misery. If too much of your weight is on the left side it's extremely difficult to make a wide backswing. This is likely to restrict your weight transfer – and perhaps even cause a destructive reverse pivot where you lean towards the target on the backswing.

If you have more than half of your

THE WEIGHTING GAME
Whatever your age, sex or build, making sure your weight distribution is correct benefits your game. Most of your weight must be on the left foot through impact. This action helps you hit down and through the ball – essential if you want the satisfaction and enjoyment of hitting crisply struck iron shots.

WEIGHT WATCHERS

1 SHARED EQUALLY
Make sure your weight is evenly distributed – position your feet about shoulder width apart for a solid base. If you get it right at address you make life easier when parts start moving. Note how the arrows show the small amount of sway needed for good weight transfer.

2 HALFWAY BACK
Sweeping the club back long and wide naturally pulls your weight away from the ball. From an evenly balanced position at address, more of your weight is on the right than the left – even at this early stage in the swing.

5 CONTROLLED POWER
A good weight shift helps generate power at impact. The left leg is firm and supporting more than half your body weight. Both arms are fully extended, driving the clubhead low towards the target. The ball is propelled forward on a penetrating flight.

6 RIGHT TO LEFT
The body faces the target and the left leg is straight – note the position of the right foot indicating how little weight is on that side. When the weight transfer is as smooth as this you can maintain perfect control from start to finish.

3 TOP OF BACKSWING
Notice how the head has tilted slightly to allow an uninhibited shoulder turn, yet it has moved sideways very little from its original position. If your head does move too far, there's every chance something else in the swing has also done so.

4 SMOOTH DOWN
The shift of weight back towards the target should start before you pull the club down. This helps set the club on the correct path down into the ball and also guards against flailing with your hands only.

weight on the right side at address there's every chance you sway too far away from the ball on the backswing.

RIGHT FROM THE START

Your backswing is the key move. A wide takeaway acts as a trigger to help you transfer your weight on to the right side. Achieve this and you naturally pull your upper body into a coiled position.

Your right leg acts as a brace at the top of the backswing. The leg should be comfortably flexed yet firm to resist any tendency to sway backwards. This puts you in a strong position to support your body weight.

Think of tempo at the top and make sure you transfer your weight smoothly towards the left side on the downswing. As well as promoting a pure strike, it helps you achieve the classic balanced followthrough so recognizable with good golfers.

If you leave your weight trailing behind, you probably find yourself scooping at impact. It's impossible to strike correctly if you're toppling

back away from the ball. The likelihood is you hit plenty of thinned shots.

When you analyse your swing, remember that weight transfer is not the same as a sway. It's important to understand the difference between the two.

A very slight sway away from the ball on the backswing is fine and encourages weight transfer. So if you study your swing in a mirror or on video, don't feel anxious if you do sway a little on the backswing. The important point is that your weight shifts towards the ball on the way down. An excessive sway is potentially disastrous – it's definitely a problem that must be addressed.

TRANSFER TRAINING

A simple exercise can help you appreciate the importance of weight transfer. When you're next on the practice ground, adopt your normal stance with your weight equally distributed on both feet. A 5 iron is the best club to use.

Hit a couple of shots while making a deliberate attempt to keep your

feet firmly planted on the ground – almost as if there's glue on the soles of your shoes. This makes it impossible to transfer your weight correctly during the swing – particularly through impact. You're certain to hit al-most every bad shot imaginable so don't continue this drill for too long.

Now revert to a more orthodox action. Concentrate on transferring your weight on to the right foot on the backswing and on to the left on the downswing. Straight away you should strike the ball with more power and authority.

pro tip

Supporting role
An accurate way to check you're in a good followthrough position is to try to stand on your left leg immediately after you complete your swing. If you can, it means your balance is good and that you're transferring your weight correctly both on the downswing and through impact.

Perfecting your balance

The golf swing is an exercise that has an uncanny knack of upsetting an otherwise impeccable sense of balance. Staying firmly planted on your own two feet sounds simple enough, but it still manages to elude many club players.

The fault is so common because many golfers regard balance as an unimportant aspect of the swing – therefore they don't feel the need to work on it. They're so tied up with straight left arm, head down and coiled upper body that they forget about the movement of their feet and overall balance. It's an attitude that cannot possibly produce consistent results.

Don't make striking the ball more difficult than it already is. Be sure that you pay at least as much attention to perfecting your balance as you do to any other part of the swing.

ON AN EVEN FOOTING

There are times when keeping your balance is not easy, so you need to know how to cope. Even golfers who appear rock solid over the ball and during the swing can be prone to a slight wobble. Wild and windy days on an exposed links are often the cause of the problem – gusting breezes buffet you as you fight to stay steady.

In these testing conditions you need to work doubly hard at maintaining your balance – not just over the full shots but from close range too.

Widen your stance a fraction to give yourself a more solid foundation over the ball. Shorten your swing to make it more compact and less vulnerable to a battering from the wind – this has the added benefit of helping you hit the ball lower than normal.

If you have a long, willowy swing you're especially likely to suffer from balance problems in the wind. Bear in mind that the more compact you make your swing the better it stands up in gusty conditions. Picture Ian Woosnam's swing for example. Solid, straight-forward – he's one

▶ STUMBLING BLOCK
The tell-tale signs of poor balance are easy to spot. All the body weight moves away from the target instead of flowing on to the left side. This technique destroys all hope of striking the ball correctly because the clubhead is on an upward path at impact. You're likely to block the ball out to the right. The cardinal rule of iron play is to strike down on the ball – impossible to achieve if your balance is so out of control that you topple backwards on the downswing.

◀ BALANCED FINISH
Good and bad together is an excellent combination when trying to identify specific faults. This is a fine example and highlights the benefits to be gained by keeping your balance. You can transfer your weight smoothly on to the left side which enables you to strike down and through the ball. The classic finish you achieve is an additional benefit – while it's too late to influence the path of the ball it still looks impressive.

DRIVING IN CALM CONDITIONS

1 ROCK STEADY
Even when there isn't a breath of wind you still need to concentrate hard on maintaining your balance. This is especially true when you have the driver in your hands – it's this more than any other club that causes golfers almost to throw themselves at the ball which ultimately results in a loss of balance.

2 ADDRESS TO TAKEAWAY
Sweep the club back close to the ground for at least the first 12in (30cm) of the backswing – this is one of the more popular pieces of advice because it concerns one of the most important moves in the swing. The straight line formed at address by your left arm and the shaft of the club should have altered very little at this stage of the swing.

3 SWING ACTIVATOR
This is the first clear sign of the swing starting to take shape and is a fine example of one good move leading to another. Taking the club back low to the ground sets the necessary wide arc – this in turn pulls the upper body into a coiled position and starts to shift your weight towards the right side.

4 TURNING POINT
Halfway through the swing you should feel in complete control of your balance. Whether you reach horizontal at the top of the backswing is really a matter of personal choice – a lot depends on how supple you are. Just short is a good position because it gives you time to turn fully and yet still remain in control.

5 BALANCING ACT
A smooth transfer of weight on to the left side helps you keep your balance in the hitting area. Note the good extension through the ball – clubhead speed should almost pull you into the followthrough. If ever golfers suffer from poor balance it tends to be at this stage of the swing – usually caused by a frantic lunge from the top.

6 HAPPY ENDING
This more than any other part of the swing is where you can spot the difference between good and bad balance. It's the followthrough position achieved by every professional and is something you can learn from and copy yourself. You can only finish the swing in impressive fashion like this by transferring your weight correctly and maintaining your balance.

of the finest wind players in the world.

When you have to play a shot from a viciously sloping lie, you need to counteract the imbalance by slightly altering your weight distribution.

As a rule you need to go against the slope. With the ball well below the level of your feet, shift a little more of your weight on to your heels to prevent you toppling forwards when you swing. Move your weight more towards your toes to help you cope with a ball above your feet.

BALANCE OF POWER

In calm conditions on reasonably flat ground there are no excuses for losing your balance. For the full shots you must maintain good balance because it helps you transfer your weight with control throughout the swing.

Your weight moves away from the ball on the backswing and on to the left side through impact. When you carry this out smoothly you enhance your power. But if your balance is slightly out, you upset both your rhythm and timing. This is certain to have a disastrous effect on the strike.

Perfect balance also consistently helps you keep the clubhead on the correct swing plane throughout.

When you see a golfer with poor balance, look at the direction the clubhead travels during the swing – it's unlikely to stay on the same plane from start to finish. A more likely scenario is that as the player topples from one poor position to another, the clubhead is unavoidably thrown out of plane.

Your swing plane in turn has an effect on the path of the clubhead through impact. When the plane is consistent you can more accurately control the direction of the clubhead as it meets the ball – one good move results from another earlier in the swing.

Short game stance
Windy conditions often play havoc as your ball flies through the air, but don't pretend the problems come to an end there. When you move closer to the hole there are other difficulties you need to contend with.

The key to holding your short game together in strong winds is keeping still over the ball and staying balanced. To achieve this, take every step possible to build a solid and compact stance for both your chipping and putting.

Stand with your feet slightly wider apart than normal. This establishes a good foundation and helps prevent any unwanted movement over the ball. You probably know from experience how important this can be to the shot. There's nothing more distracting than feeling a strong gust of wind just as you're about to start your takeaway.

Fall over backwards
Toppling backwards is a very common fault among handicap golfers. Sufferers are bound to be plagued by inconsistency and disappointment.

If your weight moves away from the target on the downswing you can forget about hitting the ball well – even from a good position at the top of the backswing. More often than not the shot goes horribly wrong.

The fault happens because the arc of your swing moves backwards along with you. This immediately destroys any good work you may have done earlier such as setting up to the ball correctly. As you come down there is little hope of making good contact – the clubhead either thuds into the ground before the ball, or travels up at the point of impact resulting in an ugly thinned shot.

Remember, a slight sway from the target is fine on the backswing. But you must transfer your weight on to the left side on the downswing – failure to do so can only end in poor strikes.

Beat driver phobia

Those who dread the driver and steer clear of the club at all costs are missing out on one of the most uplifting experiences in golf – a good bash with a driver bites a large chunk out of most holes and is a tremendous boost to your confidence.

The problem for a lot of golfers is not always genuine fear of hitting this club, more a case of struggling to find a driver they feel comfortable with.

If you've ever felt this way you probably take the headcover off your driver very reluctantly. It's hardly surprising that some golfers store their drivers in the cupboard rather than the golf bag.

The search for that elusive longest club in the bag is rather like looking for your perfect putter – it often takes time and can easily mean experimenting with several makes and styles.

The driver is a very personal club – far more so than any set of irons you'll ever buy. Once you find one you like, stick with it through thick and thin. The club takes on a far less frightening appearance and at times you're likely to feel you can hit almost any shot – this is very important in a pressure situation.

DRIVING LESSON

Even with a club that suits you it's important to know how to drive before you can stand on the tee with total confidence.

Although it's mainly a distance club, never hit your driver flat out unless the situation is really desperate and crying out for you to take a gamble.

The well known phrase that you

TAKE THE EASY OPTION
Every golfer drives the ball badly from time to time – even the best in the world. Don't feel you have to slog your way through a slump with your driver – if you're suffering from a bout of low confidence it could take a depressingly long time. Move down to your 3 wood and swing the club just as you would a driver. You don't lose much distance, the club is easier to hit, and an upturn in morale is just round the corner.

pro tip

TWO UMBRELLAS AT DRIVER DISTANCE

30yd (27m) APART – WIDTH OF AVERAGE FAIRWAY

Realistic aim

When you practise with your driver it's important you set yourself a realistic target to hit. Two umbrellas serve the purpose as well as anything. Stick them in the ground at the distance you hit your driver – about 30yd (27m) apart represents the width of the average fairway.

You're unlikely to hit every ball between the umbrellas, but the target at least gives you the sort of landing area you would expect to find on the course. If you're driving well you can achieve a good success rate and gradually build on your confidence. If you don't have two umbrellas, aim between two trees at the end of the practice ground – this is an equally realistic target area.

Whatever you do, don't try to pump drives at a lone pencil-thin tree in the distance. This is likely to destroy what confidence you started the day with because it's such a difficult target to hit.

TAKE YOUR TIME – SWING WITHIN YOURSELF

should swing your driver as you do a 9 iron is one of the finest single pieces of advice you can absorb.

Try to feel as though you're swinging at about 70% of full power. This gives you the distance you need and, more importantly, the control which is essential for consistently finding the fairway.

When you stand on the tee it's important to do all you can to put yourself in a positive frame of mind – how you feel over the ball makes all the difference between success and misery.

Remember, hit a good drive away and you're rewarded with a much shorter approach than if you were to play safe with a more lofted club. This is a far better mental attitude than worrying whether or not you can keep the ball out of the trees.

Other positive points are also worth drawing upon if you suffer problems with the driver:
❍ Tee the ball high enough to ensure that the ground doesn't even come into play – this helps eliminate the risk of catching the shot heavy.
❍ Select the perfect spot on the teeing area so that you have an even patch of ground and a good foundation for your swing.

HOW THE PROS DO IT

aving read all about power and accuracy, let's take a more detailed look at how the professionals do it. We start with Ian Woosnam, who despite being short strikes the ball phenomenal distances, and Mark Calcavecchia, who launches himself at the ball, followed by the elegant Anders Forsbrand, and finally powerful Sandy Lyle, who uses a 1 iron like most people use a driver. All these golfers swing differently, but all are able to deliver the clubhead squarely to the ball at speed. Tour professionals create immense leverage in the downswing, causing a delayed strike – the main reason why they hit the ball such vast distances.

Compact coil and effective leg action give Per-Ulrik Johansson a powerful strike despite his slight frame.

masterclass

Hit big with Woosnam

Little Ian Woosnam is renowned for being one of the longest hitters in golf. At just 5ft 4 in (1.65m) in height the Welshman is a prime example of a proven theory – you don't have to be tall to send the ball a long way.

Woosnam drew inspiration from other successful small golfers – for example Gary Player and fellow Welshmen Brian Huggett and Dai Rees. Player has become a legend in the game for winning championships such as the Masters, where the Augusta course favours long hitters.

SWING PLANE

When Woosnam was younger he played a lot of golf with his great friend Sandy Lyle. As he grew older, Lyle developed problems with his swing.

But the swing was not a concern for the stocky Woosnam. His short stature makes it easier for him to swing the club around his body as he is in more of an upright position than a taller player. This advantage has given him one of the simplest and most effective swings today.

SIMPLE APPROACH

Once asked to explain what he thinks before playing a shot, Woosnam said, 'I look at the target and hit the ball at it.'

This uncomplicated approach is echoed in the way he swings the club – a smooth rhythm which varies little from week to week regardless of pressure. His apparent ease in striking the ball outstanding distances has almost become his trademark.

Before playing the stroke he blocks out all other thoughts by creating a positive image in his mind of how the ball will fly to the target. His concentration and straightforward attitude prevent confusion and let him get on with the game.

Woosnam never over exerts himself when taking a shot and so avoids bad timing and miss-hitting. Although it doesn't appear

DISTANCE HITTING
Although he is not as tall as many of his rivals, Welshman Ian Woosnam is one of the longest hitters in world golf. He achieves good distance because he has perfect rhythm and weight transfer.

WOOSNAM'S SIMPLE STYLE

1 SWEEPING TAKEAWAY
This is typical of Woosnam's uncomplicated action. With knees flexed, he sweeps the club away, keeping it low to the ground. This creates a wide swing arc, which provides all the power he needs for a long drive.

2 ROTATION AND WEIGHT SHIFT
As the Welshman swings halfway back his body is beginning to rotate. His weight now starts to move across to his right foot – by the top of the backswing almost all his weight will have transferred.

3 TAKING HIS TIME
With ease and comfort, Woosnam finishes his backswing. This relaxed, fluid movement is vital for a powerful swing. Many smaller players mistakenly rush at this point, ready to thrash the ball to achieve distance.

so, he uses only three-quarters of his power when hitting the ball. This method allows his body to synchronize, letting the correct parts work at the right time.

Rhythm is probably Woosnam's greatest asset. Whether he hits a driver, 1 iron or sand wedge, his rhythm remains constant. His quality of movement combined with those famous tree trunk forearms have contributed to his success.

Ian Woosnam has the advantage of being able to play every day. Few can play that regularly, which makes the skill of timing your shots even more important.

Woosie in action
Next time you have the opportunity, go to see Ian Woosnam in action – he is one of the best golfers to learn from. Pay particular attention to the way he swings the long clubs. You can greatly improve your game by imitating his perfect tempo.

4 SWINGING THROUGH THE BALL
Woosnam is now in the classic impact position. His left arm is in control of the swing and his right side is passive. The left hip moves easily out of the way, allowing him to swing the club through the ball.

5 PERFECT BALANCE
As his head turns to watch the ball's flight, the result of Woosnam's calm approach is a perfectly balanced followthrough. He achieves this because of the fluent rhythm he applies to all his shots, from driver to wedge.

Calcavecchia's aggression

The beefy American Mark Calcavecchia is one of the most dominant figures on the US Tour. Naturally a very attacking golfer, he goes all out for birdies whenever he can. Mark's dashing style has reaped big rewards since he turned pro – he has won over $500,000 each year since 1987 and captured the Open Championship at Troon in 1989.

His cavalier approach is tempered by sound thinking. Calcavecchia never takes on a shot that's not within his capability – but he is so talented that he can play virtually every shot imaginable. The birdies flow.

POSITIVE ATTACK

Calcavecchia sets out to win and believes attack is the best way to achieve it. All too often golfers are on the defensive, trying to protect a score instead of being positive and going all out to improve it.

Many amateurs go for their shots in practice or a friendly, but freeze in a competitive round. As soon as the dreaded scorecard is tucked away in the back pocket, thoughts turn to avoiding mistakes. The result is negative and tentative play.

Follow Mark's example of all out attack to rid your game of this hesitant and damaging approach. Don't be afraid of making mistakes, but never attempt anything well beyond your scope. Calcavecchia drops shots like anyone else but his attacking play creates the birdies that cancel them out.

LET IT RIP

The US Ryder Cup player has eyes only for the flag. Once he has set himself up properly, he launches into the shot. His critics say that he swings too fast and hits the ball too hard, but in fact Mark swings with great rhythm and has fast hands generating immense power.

Hitting the ball hard is definitely not for everyone but as long as the basic technique is sound it can help some golfers cure their stiff and tentative swing. A hard rap leads to a good release through the ball instead of guiding it at the target.

Copy Calcavecchia's positive attitude if you suffer from seeing only trouble around a hole. Focus on the fairway and flag, then go in on the attack to help rid you of the negative thoughts that so often spell doom.

Mark's aggressive style runs through all departments of his game, including putting. A positive attitude from the tee and with your approach shots can bolster your confidence on and around the green, increasing your birdie strike rate.

POWER PLAY
Mark Calcavecchia is immensely strong, combining an excellent clearing of his left side with fast hands to produce a powerful late hit. His dynamic style has made him one of the fiercest competitors in world golf.

masterclass

Forsbrand's controlled power

Ever since the athletic Swede turned pro in 1981, Anders Forsbrand has been known for his monstrous hitting. Booming drives of 300yd (275m) plus were commonplace, but unfortunately good direction didn't always accompany them.

Though Anders steadily worked his way up the Order of Merit from 120th in 1983 to 8th in 1986, he never quite harnessed his power to produce winning scores. His only Tour victory from 1982 to 1990 was the '87 European Masters.

Not long after Forsbrand's first success, his coach died and the Swede's golf began to suffer. After trying a few teachers, he finally settled for David Leadbetter to help him out of the doldrums. They both knew that Anders had to curb his wayward hitting and find more control and accuracy if he was to get back to winning ways.

FOLLOW FORSBRAND

The Scandinavian is the perfect example for anyone with natural power who struggles to keep the ball on the fairway. Don't just trust to luck – it's time to sort out your swing and find more control. Be content to lose some length.

1 STABLE STANCE
For his driver the ball is positioned opposite the left heel. His stance is relaxed but stable, with his feet set at just over shoulder width apart, and his weight evenly spread. Anders aligns parallel to the ball-to-target line – a must for straight hitting.

2 PERFECT PATH
Anders takes the club away on a very wide arc and in one piece – hands, arms, shoulders and hips all move together at the start of the backswing. At the full extent of the takeaway his clubface is square and the shaft is in line with his feet.

3 FULLY COILED FOR POWER
The Swede turns on a firm right leg and is wonderfully balanced. He has continued the wide swing arc all the way to the top, and his hands are remarkably high. The club points parallel to the target line. Coiled, he can unleash a powerful downswing.

Forsbrand's power comes naturally from a wide swing arc, full body turn and fast hands. But before he started working with the Florida based coach his swing was extremely lithe and quite fast, and he was prone to getting too far ahead of the ball at impact.

The downswing started with a lateral shift of the lower body and was sometimes too forceful. Often he couldn't return the clubface square no matter how fast his hands worked.

Now Anders has a much more controlled swing, but has not stifled his natural power. He has lost 5-10% of his distance, but is now far more accurate.

In time – perhaps within a year – Anders believes that the length he has lost should come back as he becomes more confident and used to his swing.

There is less lower body movement on the downswing – his hips turn back rather than laterally shift into impact. This stops him getting too far ahead of the ball in the striking zone.

Forsbrand also has a firmer left side through impact than before, which helps keep the club swinging at the target. His present swing looks altogether more compact and less rangy. These changes finally paid off when he won the 1991 Volvo Open in Florence.

If you are a long hitter, losing some yards doesn't harm your game. The extra control and consistency you gain actually improves your chances of scoring well.

SEEK HELP

The best way to find a more solid swing is to consult a PGA qualified professional. But for immediate help go back to basics. Try to play within yourself and don't go flat out with a driver – swing with about 85% of your normal force. This automatically increases the likelihood of the clubface returning square.

4 DYNAMIC DOWNSWING
The downswing starts by pulling the hands down together with a turning back and a slight lateral shift of the hips. The lag of the clubhead behind the hands produces a powerful late hit. He keeps his right elbow tucked in to help him attack from the inside.

5 SQUARE STRIKE
Though his left side is clearing at impact it is also held firm and gives him a solid base from which to attack. A braced left leg helps him to keep the clubhead swinging through to the target and to stay square just after impact. This helps the ball fly straight.

6 EXTEND AND RELEASE
Forsbrand's left arm folds early but the extension through the ball is still full. Keeping his left arm close to his body on the throughswing naturally brings the club back on the inside and adds to his control. At the finish his weight is totally on the left side.

masterclass

Lyle's 1 iron play

Sandy Lyle has a reputation as one of the game's longest hitters. Using his awesome power he has consistently destroyed course records throughout his career. Lyle's game has had its ups – and downs, of late – but that's golf. No one doubts his prodigious power and talent.

Although Lyle is capable of regularly hitting 300yd (272m) drives, he often settles for the safety of his 1 iron. Because of his power – he hits the 1 iron about 260yd (237m) – he may reach even par 5 holes in 2 using just his irons. He sees little point in taking a risk with a driver from the tee as a miss-hit flies further into trouble.

CLUB CONTROL

Lyle uses the club even for playing into the wind because he can keep the shot low and controlled. Using just his irons from the tee in the third round at the 1987 Open at Muirfield he shot a level par 71 through horrendous weather, while others struggled with their drivers.

Sandy performs brilliantly with the 1 iron, though his swing is not best suited to hitting long clubs.

1 MODEL OF EXCELLENCE
Sandy Lyle takes up a relaxed position over the ball with a classic set-up. He is well balanced and his posture is superb. Notice how he keeps his chin up clear of his chest to allow the free passage of the left shoulder.

ACCURACY AND POWER

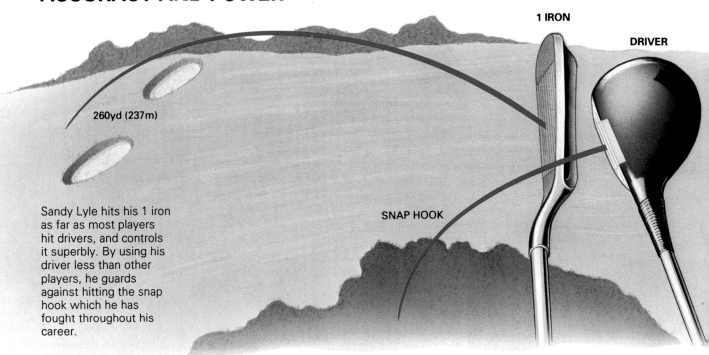

260yd (237m)

1 IRON

DRIVER

SNAP HOOK

Sandy Lyle hits his 1 iron as far as most players hit drivers, and controls it superbly. By using his driver less than other players, he guards against hitting the snap hook which he has fought throughout his career.

2 STYLE OF HIS OWN
At the halfway stage of his backswing the clubhead is slightly more to the inside of the ball-to-target line than normal. This is a legacy of his younger days when he was shorter and he swung flat, and it can lead to a snap hook.

3 SHORT AND CONTROLLED
The top of the backswing position is also far from conventional. He swings well short of the parallel and the clubhead is laid off, but it is controlled. Although his club does not reach the classic position his shoulder turn is excellent.

4 CORRECT SWING PATH
As with all great players, any flaws on the backswing are put right on the downswing. Lyle is very impressive through the ball, and he displays excellent left side control. Notice the extension through the stroke.

Because he started playing golf at an early age he developed a flattish swing plane more often used by a short person.

In his teens he shot up to 6ft 2in (1.88m) but kept a swing better suited to a golfer around 5ft 6in (1.68m). Sandy still suffers from the backswing he had when he was younger – it can cause a violent snap hook which easily puts him in trouble.

COMFORTING CONTROL

Sandy prefers the 1 iron to a 3 wood or driver because the shaft is shorter. The shorter shaft gives Lyle a comforting sense of control over the clubhead. He feels less likely to hit a poor shot – the iron doesn't produce the extremely flat swing plane that he sometimes has with a wood.

With confidence and a sound technique the 1 iron shot isn't that hard to play, but some players still prefer using a 3 wood for safety play. The main reason is the difference in appearance. There's more loft on a 1 iron than a 3 wood but the thinness of the blade is disconcerting. The lower centre of mass and the shape of the wood make it look easier to hit than the iron.

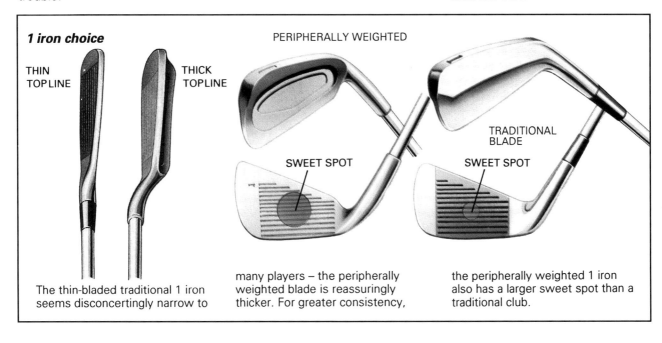

1 iron choice

THIN TOPLINE   THICK TOPLINE

PERIPHERALLY WEIGHTED

SWEET SPOT

TRADITIONAL BLADE

SWEET SPOT

The thin-bladed traditional 1 iron seems disconcertingly narrow to

many players – the peripherally weighted blade is reassuringly thicker. For greater consistency,

the peripherally weighted 1 iron also has a larger sweet spot than a traditional club.

Develop the power hit

Millions of golfers throughout the world constantly strive for more power and extra distance. Too many fail and become wild because they try to swing faster to gain more length.

Greater swing speed does not equal greater distance. Clubhead speed is the critical factor. This is generated by a combination of dynamic body action and fast hands. For maximum power you need to create a lag of the club-head behind your hands on the downswing, and release into impact at the last possible moment – the late hit.

The world's most powerful golfers are all natural late hitters and have no need to force the hands to work. But luckily you can develop this power hit to a degree – without ruining your tempo, rhythm and control.

ANGLE HELD FROM TOP OF BACKSWING UNTIL HANDS ALMOST AT IMPACT POSITION

LATE HIT GENERATES MASSIVE CLUBHEAD SPEED

110 mph

HOLD ANGLE FOR LATE RELEASE

The key to a late hit is to retain the angle – formed between your shaft and left forearm at the top of the backswing – for as long as possible on the downswing. Ideally you should not start working the wrists until your hands are almost opposite your right thigh.

This means that the clubhead has to travel a good distance in the last fraction of a second before impact to return square. This creates the massive clubhead speed needed to hit the ball powerfully.

But you must never force the hands to work – they should be free and loose. Also never leave the releasing of the hands too late as it is almost impossible for the blade to return square. The likely result of leaving it too late is a huge carve out to the right.

However good your hand action, you must still combine it with good body positions to generate maximum power and still stay in control. You can't get the best from your fast hands unless you take the club away on a wide swing arc, make a full shoulder turn and drive into the ball with your lower body.

HANDS WORK EARLY
ON DOWNSWING

BLADE SQUARE BUT
LACKS REAL CLUBHEAD
SPEED AT IMPACT

80 mph

THE SWING OF A MERE MORTAL
Most decent golfers have an element of the late hit in their swings. But most just fail to get maximum power out of their action because their hands and wrists start working into impact a fraction before the ideal point. There is nothing wrong with this action – in fact it is easier to control than a very late hitter's – but you can improve it slightly through practice.

pro tip

Power drills
Although it is difficult to teach the late hit to someone who doesn't naturally have good hands, it is still possible to develop it to some degree by using drills.
● **Downswing hold.** One simple drill helps you ingrain the feeling of the correct late hitter's downswing action into your muscle memory. Set up as normal and take a short iron to the top. Then start down concentrating on holding your wrists firm. Swing down to a point when your hands are almost opposite your right thigh. Stop.

Only hold it there for a fraction of a second – so you don't lose your rhythm – then move the club back to the top and repeat three times without ever unhinging your wrists. On the third swing continue past the stopping point and release your hands into the ball.

Keep repeating this drill. You should soon feel yourself creating a little more lag and power. Don't worry if you push the balls slightly to start with – in time you should naturally work your hands more, so that the blade returns square at impact.
● **Bell ringer.** Many teaching professionals suggest using your imagination to help develop the power hit. Think of yourself pulling down hard on a bell rope from the top of the backswing. This action of trying to ring a bell automatically makes your hands pull sharply down and keeps your wrists from working until late on helping you produce the late hit.

masterclass

Mighty Fred
If there is one golfer in the world today who perfectly illustrates the mix of an easy swing with awesome power, it has to be Fred 'Boom Boom' Couples. The distances he smacks the ball are often unbelievable, because his swing is so languid, smooth and unhurried.

The slow tempo belies the fact that Fred's hands start working into impact extremely late, and so generate enormous clubhead speed. The lag he creates is astonishing, and even when his hands are almost at their impact position, the clubhead trails way behind.

This action comes naturally and Fred never forces the shot. This means he has control to go with his might – a potent combination that has lifted Couples into the world's top rank.

Regain lost power

Knowing that you're not hitting the ball as far as you can is very frustrating. But don't despair – loss of power is easily curable if you recognize and understand the causes.

The main reason for power loss is a narrowing of the swing arc. This happens when you pick up the club too steeply with excessive wrist movement – usually because you've not turned properly. By not turning your shoulders the arms can't extend in the backswing.

This creates a narrow arc which leads to a poor top of the backswing position. The downswing also becomes narrow – reducing clubhead speed – and the follow-through is wristy with no extension. All add up to loss of power.

RECOVERING DISTANCE
Enormous power is generated through a well shaped swing. Although loss of power and distance is annoying it's easy to remedy. As an advanced player you should learn how and why power loss happens. If you understand the causes you can put the fault right – even in mid round – with some simple changes.

WIDENING YOUR ARC

1 EXTENDED TAKEAWAY
Extend your arms fully and avoid breaking your wrists too soon. You create a wide arc which carries on throughout the swing and improves both striking and length of shot. Too wristy and narrow a backswing with little shoulder turn ruins the whole swing, and power is lost (below).

2 COILED TOP OF BACKSWING
Widen your takeaway to move into a powerful position. Your right arm is tucked in, the left gently flexed. When you don't turn properly you pick the club up steeply: both arms are bent and away from the body (below) – a weak position.

3 THROUGHSWING EXTENSION

Extend fully through the ball (above). This action helps increase clubhead speed and drives the ball forward on a good trajectory. Swinging with a narrow arc means your wrists break too early (below) and the ball is flicked into the air which loses you distance.

4 HIGH BALANCED FINISH

Swinging with a wide arc naturally pulls you into a high finishing position and helps you transfer your weight fully on to the left side (above). You tend to collapse into a sloppy finish if you use a wristy narrow swing, and your weight stays on the back foot.

Set-up check

It's hard to see faults in your own game – you may think you're setting up perfectly but in reality you could have a flaw.

Ask a friend to check your set-up. It helps if you lay down a couple of clubs parallel to each other and one at right angles across them to make sure you're aligning properly and your ball position is correct.

Position the two clubs parallel to the ball-to-target line – this helps you get used to setting up correctly in relation to the flag. Place balls on the ground a shoulder width apart to encourage a correct stance.

A solid set-up helps to achieve consistent striking, and a good strike means you shouldn't lack distance.

ALIGN FEET, HIPS AND SHOULDERS PARALLEL WITH BALL-TO-TARGET LINE

BALL POSITION FOR DRIVER OPPOSITE LEFT HEEL

WIDE EXTENSION

To combat narrow swinging you must widen your arc – you may then be pleasantly surprised how far you hit the ball. Make a conscious move to take the club away in a wide arc by extending your arms as far back as possible while making a full shoulder turn. Your wrists should start to break just before the club reaches the horizontal on the backswing.

This extension helps you move into a coiled top of the backswing position. From here, unleash a powerful downswing and generate good clubhead speed. Make sure you extend fully through the ball – breaking the wrists and arms too early can lose you power. But keep your action smooth – never forsake rhythm for all out power.

SIMPLE SET-UP

Power is also lost through an incorrect set-up. Often slight faults creep into your game without you knowing it. Bad ball position or stance frequently lead to inconsistent striking and loss of distance.

Standing too close or too far away from the ball makes you hit it off centre. And your swing is

awkward, and striking difficult, if the ball is positioned too far forward or back.

Go back to the basics. Take time to set up square – check alignment and ball position. The perfect way to regain power is to swing with a smooth wide arc from a good solid set-up.

Even if your set-up is good and your swing wide, an incorrect grip

pressure can lose you length. When you're tense or if a hole is narrow, it's easy to grip the club too tightly and try to guide the ball.

You must have light grip pressure for your wrists to be free to generate clubhead speed. A light grip helps you make a full and flowing swing, improving your striking and increasing the distance you hit the ball.

Nicklaus works it out

Even the greats of the game sometimes suffer from a loss of distance. Whenever Jack Nicklaus notices that he's losing length off the tee he goes to the practice ground to work on regaining power.

In his case the loss of power usually comes from a slight narrowing of the swing arc. He deliberately extends his arms as much as possible on the backswing and therefore creates a wider arc with which he can attack the ball powerfully.

Coming to the 1980 US Open at Baltusrol, Jack found he had lost length. He worked on widening his arc – he believes this drill helped him win the event.

Build your golf muscles

Exercising the muscles you use in golf helps you hit further. It also aids control so you can achieve distance without overhitting. Even if you have a sound technique, you may not be hitting as far as you should. Building up muscles contributes to a smoother swing so your shots go further.

STRONG HANDS AND ARMS

Most top golfers are certainly not body builders – some are the opposite – but if you look at their forearms, wrists and hands you'll see they are very muscular.

Strong legs are also much in evidence, because they help to generate clubhead speed as the club is swung through the ball. Flexibility, strength and technique combine to make hitting the ball long distances easy. Strength also improves your stamina around the course.

With all strengthening exercises, repeating regularly is the key to progress. Don't start off your programme too aggressively – you could damage muscles. If you are an older player or aren't in the best of health, seek advice from a doctor first.

REGULAR ROUTINE

Work out a daily routine that suits your physique and the time you have available. Gradually increase

Stretch before you lift
Start your programme with stretching exercises before you make any attempt to lift weights. This is because stretching actions pump blood into your muscles, warming them up. Begin gently – stand on your toes and stretch your arms up as far as possible before starting work on specific parts of the body.

If you try to lift weights before your muscles are warmed up, you risk injury by loading stress on unprepared ligaments and tendons.

your exercise level and you'll start to feel the benefits. Don't try to rush – you'll cancel any positive results.

To become a good golfer your lower arms must be very strong. The hands, wrists and forearms control the club through the impact area and are responsible for the

FIT RUBBER WEIGHTS
Exercise often to strengthen your wrists and forearms. Fit rubber weights – available from your PGA pro – to the end of the shaft above the head, and swing to the top of the backswing. Stop for five seconds before swinging through, then repeat the exercise.

GOLF EXERCISES

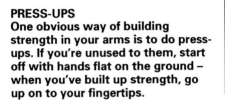

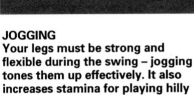

PRESS-UPS
One obvious way of building strength in your arms is to do press-ups. If you're unused to them, start off with hands flat on the ground – when you've built up strength, go up on to your fingertips.

SIT-UPS
Sit-ups are a useful all round exercise which tone the stomach and lower back. Take it slowly at first, and don't push your body beyond what feels comfortable, to avoid straining your back.

JOGGING
Your legs must be strong and flexible during the swing – jogging tones them up effectively. It also increases stamina for playing hilly courses or 36 holes a day. Always wear proper running shoes.

SWING WITH TWO CLUBS
Another way of building strength in the hands and forearms is to swing back and through as normal but with two clubs instead of one. You'll be surprised how light and fluid one club feels afterwards – and how comfortable your swing becomes.

TOUCH YOUR TOES
Touching your toes keeps your lower back muscles and the backs

of your legs supple and springy – vital for good golf. Less supple players should bend their knees.

timing of the stroke.

If yo ur lower arms are weak, you have to reduce your clubhead speed to improve your timing – which reduces distance.

Several exercises boost lower arm strength – for example, swinging a club with a weight added to the head or swinging two clubs at once are both effective.

TYRE EXERCISES

Strange as it sounds – and looks – giving a tyre a hefty whack with a club helps increase forearm strength. Your local tyre centre may give you an old tyre free of charge. Use an old club – you don't want to damage a favourite one – and gradually hit harder. Keep practising the exercise, hitting more often as you go along.

There's another useful routine with a tyre which strengthens wrists. Gripping an iron as normal, wriggle it from side to side inside the tyre – you'll be surprised how energy sapping it is, and how effectively muscles are toned.

The left arm is the leading arm for right handed golfers (right arm for left handers) as it controls the

STRENGTHEN LEADING ARM
Make your leading arm (left for right handers, right for left handers) stronger. Hold a wood in your leading hand – palm upward – and

turn your hand over so that the club faces the other way. If it proves a bit tough at first, hold halfway down the shaft and work your way up to the grip.

pro tip

Coiling a brick
You can pump up hands, wrists and arms by slowly coiling a brick attached to a length of wood by strong cord. Don't try to complete the exercise in one attempt – take it slowly.

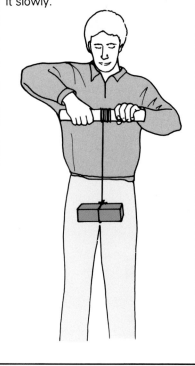

STAY SUPPLE AND TURN CORRECTLY

1 CLUB BEHIND SHOULDERS
For a supple shoulder turn place a club lengthways behind your shoulders and take your normal address posture.

2 FULL TURN
Make a full turn to the right, keeping your shoulders level throughout. Keep your movements smooth.

3 TRANSFER YOUR WEIGHT
Let your hips turn back to the left, with your weight transferring fluently through just as it does in the golf swing.

club through impact. Yet most right handers are physically stronger in their right sides.

Work on improving this lack of balance by exercising your weaker side. Swing a club with the left arm only – hit some balls once you're used to it.

FLUID MOVING PARTS

All round flexibility is important in golf – you use most of your body's moving parts in the swing. Toe touching and sit-ups are useful ways of improving suppleness – but go gently at first.

Holding a club lengthways across the back of your shoulders then turning back and through is a great way of improving your body turn – it also helps you develop the correct plane for the shoulder during the swing.

After a couple of months of regular planned exercise, your shots should start to fly further with every club – without any extra vigour on your part. Applying less force lets you achieve more control and greater consistency.

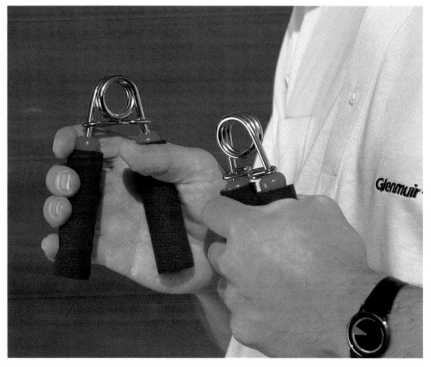

HAND GRIP
You can really build your finger, hand and lower arm strength by carrying a grip strengthener – if you don't have one, a squash ball serves the same purpose – in your pocket at all times. When you have a spare

moment – even if you're stuck in traffic – squeeze the springs.

If one side is less powerful than the other, spend more time working on the weaker side. Keep a note of the time you spend squeezing and increase it bit by bit.